A BRIEF HISTORY OF THE TITANIC

Fascinating Historical Facts of Titanic's Tragic Tale

SCOTT MATTHEWS

SCOTT MATTHEWS

A BRIEF HISTORY OF THE
TITANIC

FASCINATING HISTORICAL FACTS OF TITANIC'S TRAGIC TALE

Copyright © 2023 Scott Matthews

All rights reserved. No part of this publication may be reproduced, distributed or transmitted in any form or by any means, including photocopying, recording, or other electronic or mechanical methods, without the prior written permission of the publisher, except in the case of brief quotations embodied in critical reviews and certain other non-commercial uses permitted by copyright law.

Trademarked names appear throughout this book. Rather than use a trademark symbol with every occurrence of a trademarked name, names are used in an editorial fashion, with no intention of infringement of the respective owner's trademark. The information in this book is distributed on an "as is" basis, without warranty. Although every precaution has been taken in the preparation of this work, neither the author nor the publisher shall have any liability to any person or entity with respect to any loss or damage caused or alleged to be caused directly or indirectly by the information contained in this book.

The more that you read, the more things you will know. The more you learn, the more places you'll go. - Dr. Seuss

Contents

Introduction	ix
1. The Conception	1
2. Building the Ship	5
3. The Final Product	9
4. Sea Trials	19
5. The Maiden Voyage Begins	21
6. The Collision	27
7. The Evacuation and Sinking	33
8. The Immediate Impact	43
9. The Rescue and Response	45
10. The Aftermath	49
11. The Legacy in Media	53
12. The Cultural Impact	59
Conclusion	66
References	69

Introduction

The year is 1912 and you're one of the lucky few to set sail on a ship that can outperform any other passenger ship on the market. You settle into your room, enjoy luxurious meals, and mingle with people from all walks of society. You spend four days enjoying this routine. You spend your fifth in frigid water, slowly losing your life.

This was the fate of many passengers on the RMS *Titanic*, a passenger liner used by the White Star Line company and designated as an "RMS" (Royal Mail Ship), indicating that the vessel was authorized to carry mail under the auspices of the Royal Mail. The ship was deemed nearly unsinkable before its maiden voyage on April 10, 1912. By April 15, it was proven that this statement was completely false. Over half of the passengers on the ship died during the accident.

Those who survived were extremely traumatized but were eager to be able to tell their stories. Society mourned with them, hosting memorials and museums that continue to be funded.

These stories have captivated society since the sinking. Movies have been made about the incident. Attempts have been made to visit the remains of the shipwreck. However, few know the full story behind the ill-fated ship.

The disaster itself was entirely preventable and the results of the sinking could have been avoided with additional preparation. Panic and chaos led to more deaths than the actual sinking. Industry standards of the time were also partially to blame. The story is one full of regret and sadness, yet is also an important cautionary tale of hubris and excess.

The Conception

The RMS *Titanic* began as a project involving a trio of ships. A company named the White Star Line, headquartered in Belfast, Ireland, decided to create triplet ships, all meant to be the most powerful and luxurious on the seas. Never meant to stand alone, the RMS *Titanic* was planned to be partnered with two sister ships, the RMS *Olympic* and the RMS *Britannic*.

This was due to a desire to outperform the rivals of the White Star Line company. Cunard, another

British company, had recently built the *Lusitania* and the *Mauretania*. These ships were deemed to be the fastest passenger ships in creation. Two other companies based in Germany, Hamburg America and Norddeutscher Lloyd, were also attempting to create boats to compete with the Cunard ships. Cunard, Hamburg America, and Norddeutscher Lloyd all posed a serious threat to the White Star Line. The White Star Line feared that they could gain unbeatable prestige if they succeeded in building epic ships and went unchallenged.

Knowing that it would be difficult to beat the Cunard ships in terms of speed, White Star Line decided to focus on building ships of immense size and comfort.

The trio of boats also played an important role in improving the White Star Line's ships. The existing fleet required the use of four ships to meet industry demand. These vessels, namely the RMS *Teutonic*, the RMS *Adriatic*, the RMS *Majestic*, and the RMS *Oceanic*, were slated for retirement and replacement as their technology became obsolete.

These factors led to a discussion between the White Star Line's chairman, J. Bruce Ismay, and J.P. Morgan, the company's American-based financier who owned the company under which White Star Lines operated, known as the International

Mercantile Marine Company. During this discussion, the desire to create a new trio of boats led to the conception of the *Titanic*. The ship was to be named after the Titans found in Greek mythology. These beings were the forefathers of the gods and goddesses. They were known for their size and power. The ship was meant to mirror them in these aspects. It would be paired with the *Britannic* and the *Olympic*.

The shipbuilding company Harland & Wolff was hired to complete the project. Their long-term relationship with White Star Lines made them an obvious first choice. Wilhelm Wolff would create the initial design of the ship and Edward James Harland would perfect the model. The men were told to spend whatever was necessary to make the ships as great as they could be. Ultimately, a loose limit of three million dollars was established for the first two ships. This limit was negotiable and flexible, however. Additions were to be made as necessary.

Harland and Wolff put numerous other designers to work on the project. The Olympic line of ships was simply too important to be designed by two men alone. Lord Pirrie acted as the director of the project. Thomas Andrews, a renowned naval architect, also acted as managing director. Edward Wilding calculated the measurements of the ship's design and Alexander Carlisle was put in charge as chief draughtsman. Carlisle was to primarily work on the more ornamental portions of the ships. However, he was also put in charge of creating a reliable lifeboat system.

The design was presented to the White Star Line executives in July 1908. It was approved quickly and three letters of agreement were written. Thus, construction began shortly afterward.

Building the Ship

Building the *Titanic* was a task that took over two years to complete, beginning on March 31, 1909, and concluding in April 1912, at the Harland & Wolff shipyard in Belfast, Northern Ireland. The construction of the ship could not even begin until the company created a way to lift the necessary materials. No ship of such a size had been made before. In fact, it was said that no object of that size had been created before.

This led to the creation of two special slipways—boat ramps that enable vessels to move in and out of the water. Harland & Wolff designed these slipways with special features, including a floating crane capable of lifting incredibly heavy objects onto the ships while remaining afloat. To construct these slipways, three smaller ones had to be demolished. The new slipways could only be built using a special gantry that stood over 228 feet (sixty-nine meters) tall.

The keel was constructed first, acting as a foundation for the ship. The strong, metal hull was then built around it. The ship also held four large, visible funnels. Some of these funnels, however, were artificial. This was an attempt to mimic the powerful appearance of the competition.

The hull contained sixteen compartments that were built to be waterproof. The idea was that if one compartment was damaged, water would only enter that one area. This was supposed to allow the ship to remain afloat despite the damage—at least for a period that allowed for an emergency exit via lifeboat.

The ship was built with 159 furnaces aboard. These furnaces pumped fuel through twenty-nine boilers and onward through the engine. To house the fuel, coal bunkers were built into the ship as well. The bunkers could hold over six thousand tons of coal if necessary. The ship was also fitted with two side anchors and a center anchor. The center anchor was the largest hand-forged anchor at the time, weighing sixteen tons.

During the construction of the ship, eight people died due to the dangers of the job. This would become a mere fraction of the deaths the ship would eventually cause. In addition to the deaths, over two hundred people suffered injuries on the work site. Twenty-eight were considered to be particularly severe.

The Final Product

The result was a ship 885 feet (270 meters) long, 173 feet (fifty-three meters) tall, and ninety-two feet (twenty-eight meters) wide. There were seven decks on the ship and numerous different rooms. In addition, it was also outfitted with electric elevators to take passengers from floor to floor. The ship had many amenities, such as a sun deck and a gymnasium. Other features included officer quarters, a post office, an inquiry office, and a saloon.

Certain areas were intended to only be accessible to specific classes of guests based on the cost of their tickets. In addition, certain amenities were not available to the lower classes. For example, while first-class passengers were able to use multiple elevators, second-class passengers could only use one specific elevator. Meanwhile, third-class passengers did not have access to an elevator at all and had to use the stairs. First-class passengers also had access to a variety of eateries and shops that other passengers were unable to use. They also were placed on higher floors than second and third-class passengers, allowing more access to open decks.

The third-class passengers were left to deal with the most unfortunate parts of sea travel. Their rooms and amenities were focused along the stern and bow. This meant that any ocean turbulence would be primarily felt in these areas, making third-class passengers most likely to fall victim to sea sickness.

In addition, the quarters of the third class were the lowest on the ship. This was partially due to the need to distribute weight in this area as the small size of the rooms meant that more materials for walls would be utilized. The second-class floor was placed above it, and the first-class floor was above both. Ultimately, the third-class floor would weigh more than the second-class floor. The second class would weigh more than the first, but less than the third. Having the floors placed in this manner led to a more stable ship.

At the very bottom of the ship, all of the hard machinery could be located. In an area called the Tank Top, one could find all manner of metal. Boilers, water tanks, engines, bunkers for coal, and generators were kept here. They were attached to the floor via metal securing that prevented them from being jostled by the movements of the sea. Some of this machinery ascended above the floor, despite the floor being the tallest on the ship. These machines intersected randomly with the rooms above, making the layout of the ship somewhat puzzling without prior knowledge of the design.

The Orlop Decks were located above the Tank Top. The Lower Orlop Deck was only used to store heavy cargo. The Upper Orlop Deck held both cargo and other necessities. This deck was split in two by the machines below. The forwardmost part of the deck and the backmost were not at all attached in a manner that allowed easy travel between the areas. One had to use the higher levels of the ship to cross from one part to another.

The forwardmost part of the Upper Orlop Deck was another cargo hold. This portion of the ship was meant to be able to carry automobiles. The backmost part held primarily food. This part of the deck had refrigerators and freezers to hold perishable items.

The next level was known as the Lower Deck. This floor was similarly divided into two and could not be fully navigated without climbing to a higher floor. The forwardmost part of this floor was a place that held lodgings for workers and third-class passengers. In addition, this area also held the belongings of second and first-class passengers. This floor also had a post office and a squash court. The squash court was also fitted with a special staircase that led to the saloon several floors above. The backmost area of the Lower Deck was a mix of third-class lodging and storerooms.

The Middle Deck was next. Unlike the decks below, this deck was not split. Most of this deck consisted of third-class cabins with some second rooms mixed in. Several minor amenities like laundry rooms and third-class dining areas were located on this floor, as well as some staff lodging and second-class cabins.

The next floor was called the Upper Deck. The bow of this deck consisted of third-class cabins. The starboard side held some first-class cabins, while the middle area consisted primarily of worker lodgings and some second-class cabins.

The Saloon Deck was above the Upper Deck. Crew cabins, the third-class promenade, first-class lodgings, the Grand staircase, and the main reception hall were all located on this deck. The second-class dining hall, the first-class dining hall, the main kitchens, some second-class lodgings, and a small number of third-class lodgings were also found on this deck.

The deck above the Saloon Deck was called the Shelter Deck. It consisted of crew cabins, a crew dining room, the galley, the second-class library, the second-class promenade, the third-class lounge, some first-class rooms, and some extra rooms for the maids and servants of the first-class passengers.

Above the Shelter Deck was the Bridge Deck. Ironically, the deck did not contain a bridge but instead had many first-class rooms. Some of these rooms were fanciful suites with lounges and private promenades. There were additional rooms available for the servants of the individuals in the suites. In addition, a first-class restaurant and cafe were also placed on this deck. Apart from these amenities, a second-class smoking area and promenade were also placed here.

The Promenade Deck, reserved entirely for first class, was above the Bridge Deck. Most of this deck was built to be an open-air promenade. Some rooms were placed here, however. These rooms included various lounges, a writing room, and a few rooms for lodging. Above this deck was the Boat Deck, which housed a large amount of the crew and some first-class passengers. This deck also contained the technologies responsible for operating the lifeboat mechanism.

The ship had three engines: two steam engines and a Parson's turbine. The two steam engines had a horsepower of 30,000 when combined. The exposed outer portion of the ship was made from pine and teak, while inside a lot of the ship was covered in cork to help absorb excess moisture. The *Titanic* also had a huge rudder, which was seventy-eight feet (twenty-four meters) long. It was powered by two steering engines. In addition, the boat had a plumbing system that relied on obtaining water at port as well as an emergency distillation system that allowed seawater to be made into freshwater. The ship also contained a heating system and a radiotelegraph system.

There were twenty lifeboats on the ship. The first type, known as standard, had a capacity of up to sixty-five passengers each, with fourteen of these boats on board. The second type, collapsible, could hold up to forty-seven people each, and there were four collapsible lifeboats. Finally, there were two lifeboats known as cutters, which could hold up to forty people each. These boats were attached to davits, special cranes used to lower lifeboats. While there were sufficient davits to accommodate more than enough lifeboats for over four thousand passengers if needed, the company decided to install only enough to carry one-third of the expected passengers on the ship. This technically was acceptable under the regulations of the time, which only required boats over 10,000 tons to carry enough lifeboats for nine-hundred-ninety passengers. The lifeboats on the *Titanic* could carry just over one thousand. This was due to the idea that lifeboats were meant to be reused in an emergency; the boats would carry passengers to another larger rescue boat and then get more passengers from the troubled ship.

There were 833 rooms for first-class passengers, 614 rooms for second-class passengers, and over one thousand rooms for third-class passengers. Lodgings for crew members almost reached one thousand rooms. The rooms were modeled after high-class hotels ashore, featuring common architectural styles such as Renaissance, Empire, and Louis XV.

First-class passengers had access to a variety of rooms and activities, including their own squash court, a large saltwater swimming pool, various lounges, special restaurants, a Turkish bath with a steam room and massage facilities, a designated smoking room, and a reading and writing lounge. These amenities were fancily decorated. *A Cafe* Parisien and a *Veranduh Cafe* were also available. These cafes served coffee and light refreshments in the style of popular cafes in other countries.

Third-class passengers had fewer recreational amenities but enjoyed better lodging compared to most other ships at the time. While some open dormitory-style lodging was available, small cabins were also provided for third-class passengers. Although they didn't have access to the fancier recreational areas, they could use social gathering spaces, a smoking room, and their own reading area.

Sea Trials

Eight days before the maiden voyage, the sea trials of the *Titanic* began. Approximately 110 workers were on board during these trials, with over half being greasers and firemen, and the rest consisting of general crew members. Representatives from several companies, including those from Harland & Wolff, also participated in these trials. Two men served as radio operators, and a surveyor from the Board of Trade joined to ensure the ship's suitability for use.

The trials were not a simple trip but involved various maneuvers and movements that had to be executed in a specific way. The boat's different speeds, turning, and stopping abilities were tested both in Belfast Lough and later in the Irish Sea. The onboard surveyor signed off on the ship, declaring it seaworthy for the next twelve months.

The Maiden Voyage Begins

The *Titanic* departed from the port of Southampton on April 10, 1912, intending to cross the Atlantic Ocean. The plan was to reach New York and then return via Plymouth, England. The ship would complete this journey every three weeks, rotating with other ships in the White Star Line. This arrangement provided individuals access to the route each week.

The maiden voyage was manned by a crew of 885 individuals. Captain Edward John Smith, one of the most praised captains in the employ of the White

Star Line, led the crew. In addition to the primary crew employed long-term by the White Star Line, a significant portion of the group comprised workers who signed up just days before departure. These individuals were laborers willing to undertake a variety of available tasks.

Sixty-six individuals worked on the deck, while 325 were assigned to the engines. The remaining crew members comprised the Victualling department, responsible for preparing food and linens and attending to the passengers' needs. Of the crew, only twenty-three were women, with the majority serving as stewardesses. Additionally, a significant portion of the crew hailed from Southampton, while only a small percentage traveled from elsewhere to be part of the voyage.

Regarding passengers, the *Titanic* was under capacity for its maiden voyage. Due to a coal strike, many ships were unable to maintain their schedules during this time, prompting individuals to postpone their trips to avoid unforeseen issues. Fortunately, the coal strike ended just days before the *Titanic* set sail. However, this left little time for people to purchase additional tickets. Ultimately, about 1,300 passengers bought tickets for the maiden voyage, constituting approximately one-third of the ship's carrying capacity. It is believed that a handful of passengers were unable to make the trip, further reducing the number.

The coal strike also affected the *Titanic*. The ship could only set sail because the White Star Line allocated coal from its other vessels for the *Titanic's* voyage. Without the availability of these other ships, the voyage would have had to be postponed.

The tickets for the voyage were expensive. Third-class passengers spent $80 on the trip, equivalent to about $857 today. Meanwhile, first-class tickets often cost as much as $932, which would be around almost $100,000 today.

Passengers began arriving at the dock in Southampton around 9:30 am on April 10, 1912. Third-class passengers boarded first as they outnumbered the passengers of other classes. The other two classes boarded closer to the time of departure. Captain Smith greeted the first-class passengers as a special luxury. Meanwhile, third-class passengers underwent special inspections to ensure they were not harboring diseases that could be brought to the United States.

The ship set sail at noon with 920 passengers on board, and almost immediately after beginning the journey, an incident occurred. The *Titanic* passed close to two smaller docked vessels, the SS *City of New York* and the *Oceanic*. Its massive displacement caused both smaller ships to be lifted by a surge of water and then dropped suddenly, resulting in the snapping of one of the SS *City of New York's* mooring cables and causing it to swing toward the *Titanic* stern-first. A nearby tugboat, the *Vulcan*, came to the rescue by taking control of the SS *City of New York* and averting a collision by just four feet (1.2 meters). This incident resulted in a one-hour delay for the *Titanic*.

The ship began its journey through the English Channel, picking up passengers and eventually intending to cross the Atlantic to arrive in New York in five days. The first stop was in Cherbourg, a French port where 274 passengers boarded the ship. Additional passengers joined later when the ship arrived at Cork Harbour in Queenstown. The ship followed the Irish coast for fifty-five miles (eighty-seven kilometers) before traveling another 1,600 miles (2,719 kilometers) to reach the southeast portion of Newfoundland, referred to as "the corner."

As the ship approached this area, Captain Smith received several warnings. Other ships in the Grand Banks area had observed drifting ice, and various passengers also pointed out visible ice floating in the water. Captain Smith initially disregarded the warnings. Instead of slowing down, the ship blasted ahead at full speed.

This action was not considered a risk. During this era of maritime travel, drifting ice was deemed a challenge for those responsible for keeping watch for signs of danger. Ships were expected to proceed quickly despite the potential danger, relying on keen eyes to spot anything particularly troublesome before it escalated into a real issue. In addition, ice rarely damaged large vessels to a degree that posed any true concern. Many ships struck ice and completed their journeys with nothing more than a slight time delay. It was rare for ice to pose a true risk to a ship.

However, after the RMS *Baltic* reported further concerns about ice, Captain Smith did attempt to change course. He believed that by sailing more towards the south, he could avoid the large pieces of ice other ships were seeing. Unfortunately for him, the ice was everywhere including the southern area of the location. The SS *Amerika* reported this fact on the radio, but the message never reached the *Titanic's* captain. Several more messages were sent out around this time, emphasizing the amount of ice present.

The radio operator, however, failed to take note of these messages. He was busy aiding passengers in sending and receiving messages, as the passenger radio set had been broken the day before. There were numerous messages to be sent and received. The radio operators likely focused their attention on this issue rather than the ice warnings. The operator, Jack Phillips, made a final flaw upon receiving the last message of the night. The *Californian* reported ceasing movement for the night due to the large amount of ice surrounding the area. Phillips told the messenger to "shut up" as he was busy with other tasks. During this time, most passengers had begun retiring to their cabins, unaware of the nearby danger.

The Collision

At the time of the collision, two men were manning the crow's nest at the order of First Captain, William Murdoch. These men, Frederick Fleet and Reginald Lee, sat in freezing temperatures, looking outward as the ship trudged ahead. The water was eerily still, a sign that indicated the presence of floating ice. The stillness of the water made icebergs harder to spot, as the wave patterns normally made such objects more visible when crashing into them.

The lookouts also lacked the proper gear. An issue at their initial docking place meant they didn't even have binoculars with them, although experts claim that binoculars of the time would not have worked in darkness anyway. The two did notice an odd fog on the horizon when entering into a territory called "Iceberg Alley." Experts claim this was a mirage due to the mixing of warm and cold air that effectively blinded the duo from being able to see further into the area.

Despite the vision disturbances, Frederick Fleet did spot an iceberg at 11:37 pm. He called in a warning to Sixth Officer, James  Moody, who then attempted a maneuver to miss the iceberg. The attempted maneuver involved moving the ship's tiller (a lever attached to the rudder) to the starboard position, swinging the ship in the opposite direction by moving the bow first and then the stern. A slight time delay on the orders mixed with a failure to reverse the center turbine and propeller led to a slowed movement. Had the ship not been too slow, there is a chance that the iceberg could have been avoided, although this chance was still relatively low in likelihood.

A direct collision was avoided, but the ship sideswiped the iceberg. Underwater ice scraped against the ship as the engines stopped. The ship began to drift south slowly and the hull ripped open in a non-connecting line. Some areas had larger rips than others, but the overall damage spanned 300 feet (ninety-one meters). Later, six openings created by the iceberg would be counted. These openings were located where the hull plates normally sat, suggesting they may have been forced off the ship during the collision. This could be attributed to the brittleness of the rivets holding the plates in place. The specific type of rivet used became even more brittle in cold waters, making them prone to snapping and shattering.

While people assumed a large hole had been created in the ship, this was untrue. The damage was small and seemed innocuous until the ship began to take on water. There was no sign of damage above the waterline. Passengers only felt a minor bump when the iceberg hit. Nobody suspected anything was amiss. Yet, water immediately began to flow into the ship at seven tons per second. This was over a dozen times faster than it could be removed via pump.

Two workers, James Hesketh and Frederick Barrett, were the first to be struck by icy water. Despite working near boilers, they managed to escape their work quarters safely. Boilers tended to explode when touched by freezing water. A watertight door mechanism prevented this, but in turn, risked locking workers inside the flooding rooms. Workers began to vent the steam and lower the fires to further reduce the risk of an explosion. The ship flooded so rapidly that they were wading in ice water by the time they finished their task.

The lower decks relied on bulkheads to separate various compartments and keep water from flowing from one to another during emergencies. Unfortunately, these bulkheads did not have a full seal on the top. If water flowed too high in one compartment, it would spill over to the next. This was exactly what happened when the ship began to flood. While the ship could still float with up to two flooded compartments, it could not float with the rapid flooding of almost all lower decks. Upon discovering the flooding, Captain Smith sought the opinion of builder Thomas Andrews, who noted that at least five compartments were flooded, and the ship would sink. There was nothing to be done other than evacuate. He stated that the ship had about two hours left before sinking.

During these two hours, the ship flooded in an inconsistent and unpredictable manner. It began to tilt vertically, slowly tilting a few degrees at a time until suddenly it rapidly sank in one direction.

The Evacuation and Sinking

It was shortly after midnight on April 15 when Captain Smith had the passengers informed of the collision. Stewardesses were told to alert each cabin and have them gather on the upper decks. First-class passengers received additional assistance in gathering belongings as the stewardesses had fewer cabins to attend to. Second and third-class passengers received a rapid rousing. The doors would swing open and stewardesses would shout for them to prepare to head to the upper decks.

Some passengers refused to leave their cabins. They did not believe that they were in real danger. This was compounded by the lack of information given. Nobody was directly told that the ship was sinking. Many assumed a lesser concern was at play and did not want to waste their time braving the cold for something minor.

At this time, the crew also began preparing the twenty lifeboats. Sixteen standard lifeboats were attached to davits on each side, with 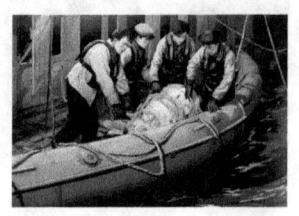 eight on each. Additionally, two collapsible lifeboats were positioned underneath some of the wooden boats, while two more were located above the officers' quarters. The logistics of launching the collapsible boats relied on the davits being free from any other lifeboats, and using the lifeboats on top of the officers' cabins would be even more challenging, as they would need to be manually carried to the davits.

There were not enough boats to carry everyone to safety at once. Instead, another ship was needed to take passengers off of the boats so that the lifeboats could be sent back to get more passengers. No other ship was in the immediate area. The radio operators began sending out calls for help, but an error of fifteen miles (twenty-four kilometers) in location led them to the wrong spot. The reason that there were so few lifeboats was due to a desire to have a promenade with an unobstructed view. More lifeboats meant compromising the beautiful view, which the designers of the ship refused to consider. Thus, without the aid of an additional ship, survival would be difficult.

About fifteen minutes later, stewardesses gave additional commands to passengers. People were told to fasten their life belts. Once again, many refused to comply. Some began to play around with the ice that had accumulated on the ship. Captain Smith began to realize the gravity of the situation. He had only enough lifeboats for a portion of his passengers. His ship was sinking. If no other ship came to help, they would all die in the icy water. On top of that, his passengers did not even realize the danger they faced. Despite this, he reacted calmly and took charge of the situation.

Smith began assessing the damage immediately. He also began to prepare the various crew members for the tasks they were about to undertake. The crew was preparing lifeboats before he was informed that the ship was indeed sinking, and most passengers had already been given instructions. Smith helped various crew members with their tasks while also helping wrangle the more feisty of the passengers. While he did his best to help the situation, the rest of the crew was dangerously underprepared. They had received little to no lifeboat training and communication was not happening as clearly or quickly as Smith would like.

Before the voyage, only a simplistic lifeboat drill had been run. Less than twenty crew members participated, and it consisted of simply lowering the lifeboats into the water. Herding passengers, loading the boats, lowering the boats with the weight of the passengers, and steering the boats were not part of the drill. While crew members were given an assigned lifeboat to work with, few knew their actual assignment. Those who did were unaware of how to operate the davits and were not trained in rowing. The crew was so underprepared that not all of the initial sixteen standard lifeboats were launched before the ship fully sank. Having a larger number of lifeboats likely would not have even solved the issues faced by the crew and passengers. In addition, minimal supplies were placed on each lifeboat despite initial plans for emergency provisions, making rescue an even more immediate necessity. Those who managed to successfully flee the sinking ship had almost no supplies or food.

Women and children were ordered to be the first loaded into the lifeboats. One of the officers in charge began lowering boats with some empty seats into the water,  interpreting the order to mean that no men should be allowed into the lifeboats, even if no more women or children were present to take a seat. The other officer, First Officer Murdoch, allowed men to take seats if all nearby women and children had already been seated. A lot of passengers refused to enter the lifeboats in the early stages of the sinking, assuming that the situation was not a true emergency. When the first lifeboat departed, it had only twenty-eight of its sixty-five seats filled. Ten minutes later, another lifeboat holding only twenty-eight passengers was lowered on the opposite side. No lifeboat, except for number eleven, reached full capacity before descending; it exceeded its allotted capacity by five people.

 In addition to the low number of people who managed to escape via lifeboats, there were other issues with them. Some boats got jammed or bumped into the ship on the way

down, resulting in many passengers suffering minor to moderate injuries during the descent. Women were emotionally injured at having to leave behind their husbands, many of whom would die on the sinking ship. The husbands had to plead with their wives to board the lifeboats, as many of the wives initially refused to leave. Some couples decided to die together. Many sat on deck chairs, holding hands and waiting for the end.

While a significant part of the crew worked to persuade passengers to board the lifeboats, and another segment attempted to man the boats, other crew members were compelled to maintain basic ship operations. Steam had to continue to be vented from boilers, pumps had to be used to remove water when possible, and generators had to be maintained to ensure the ship had electricity. Many crew members perished while attempting to manage these operations. Some were crushed by buckling portions of the ship, while others drowned in the icy waters, and some were swept out to sea, never to be found.

Flooding in the boiler rooms suggested that a hole had likely been created under the ship. The remaining unflooded boiler rooms had to be manned to prevent the ship from exploding. The men in these rooms stayed throughout the sinking and died there. Through their sacrifices, the ship was able to continue to run the lights and send out distress calls, saving more lives. In addition to these crew members, several postal clerks also died in the mail room, attempting to save important parcels.

Some of the crew did manage to escape their stations in the ship towards the end of the sinking. However, by the time they reached the upper deck, the lifeboats had all left. They stood with several engineers, watching the ship sink.

Many third-class passengers also died due to their cabins being on the lower floors. The flooding began quickly and worsened rapidly. While some were able to escape, many died in their cabins. This was partially due to the system of gates and hallways that the third-class passengers had to navigate. These passageways purposefully helped keep the classes from mingling to adhere to international travel laws, but they led to the deaths of many passengers. Some accounts state that the crew intended for this to happen.

Some crew members locked gates and doors, preventing third-class passengers from escaping. They even guarded open hallways, obstructing evacuation. This seemed to be an attempt to reserve lifeboats for first-class and second-class passengers. However, one stewardess, John Edward Hart, defied protocol and made multiple trips downward to escort third-class passengers to safety.

Many of the third-class passengers who could not escape died in their rooms. Some who could escape chose not to for reasons that are still unexplained. A large group of third-class passengers died in prayer after meeting in the dining hall. They chose to pray in their last moments rather than scramble for an exit that may not exist. Others seemed to want to leave but did not attempt to do so. It is believed that they were waiting for direct commands, having become used to following orders and not thinking for themselves. Most of these individuals died holding their bags and possessions.

Distress flares were being shot every ten minutes and the radio operators continued to send out distress codes. Several ships heard the message, but no good options for rescue were available. The RMS *Carpathia* was less than sixty miles (ninety-six kilometers) away but was such a slow-moving ship that it would not arrive until long after the *Titanic* had sunk. The SS *Mount Temple* tried to help but had to stop due to the large amount of ice in the area. The SS *Californian* saw the distressed rockets being shot, yet the captain decided to ignore the signal. It was less than fifteen miles (twenty-four kilometers) away from the *Titanic*.

As the last lifeboats began to be lowered, passengers began to act erratically. A group of men attempted to force themselves into lifeboat number fourteen as it was already in the process of being lowered. One of the ship's officers had to fire warning shots in the air to spook the group into compliance. Meanwhile, lifeboat number two was discovered with two immigrants inside. An officer forced them out at gunpoint so that other passengers could board the boat. It was not even halfway full when it was lowered without the two immigrant men inside. It was also reported that an officer, believed to be Murdoch, shot several men attempting to board a lifeboat before taking his own life.

At this point, the captain declared that the time for rescue was over. It was every man for himself. Many believe he went down with the ship, while others claim he jumped into the icy water and perished. The ship's designer, Thomas Andrews, made no attempt to leave the boat. Instead, he spent some of his last moments having a cigar in the smoking room, contemplating his failure. He then tried to aid in the rescue by throwing deck furniture to survivors overboard so that they had something to float on.

Thomas Byles, a priest, was giving last rites and hearing confessions from the remaining passengers at this point. The band continued playing lively tunes as the ship sank for the remaining passengers and crew.

Soon, the ship's angle rapidly began to shift. The ship began to flood quicker than before and continued sinking downward as many people were taken by the waves. Two groups attempting to launch the last collapsible boats almost perished this way, but most ended up managing to launch the boat and board it successfully.

At this point, the ship was at a forty-five-degree angle and a large groaning noise pierced the night. This noise is believed to be the sound of the boilers bursting and various parts of the ship collapsing inward. Simultaneously, the electricity on the ship finally went out, plunging everything into darkness. People started falling off the deck and into the water. Suddenly, the ship began to rip apart, flooding even more rapidly than before. It sank fully two hours and forty minutes after the collision with the iceberg.

The Immediate Impact

The sea was filled with debris from the sunken ship. The survivors were all stranded, some in lifeboats, some on pieces of floating debris, and some wading in the icy water. The temperature of the sea at this time was twenty-eight degrees Fahrenheit (negative two degrees Celcius). Many of the individuals submerged in the water perished quickly due to cardiac arrest. Others drowned due to the effects of the cold shock response on their bodies.

A fortunate few were given spots in lifeboats, although hundreds more could have fit. A handful made it onto a collapsible lifeboat that had been improperly launched, causing it to hold frozen water. The occupants had to sit in the water for hours and some succumbed to hypothermia in the process. As the lifeboats began to row away from the scene, those in the water began calling for help.

Amidst the cries and wails, the sounds from those submerged in the water were particularly harrowing. Many in the lifeboats had assumed that everyone successfully boarded one before the ship sank. However, hearing the cries of those in the water shattered that illusion, prompting them to wonder how many individuals perished. Unfortunately, the boats did not return for those in the water, fearing they would be swarmed and capsize. Over an hour, the cries slowly faded away as those wading in the water died. Those on the boats could only wait for rescue, but some died due to the cold or falling overboard and drowning. The rest endured without any food or water until help arrived.

The Rescue and Response

It was four in the morning when the survivors were finally rescued. The RMS *Carpathia* had successfully located the site of the wreck after spending the night dodging icebergs in a high-speed race to the rescue. Thirty minutes before the ship's arrival, it became visible to survivors. This provided many of them with a final boost of strength to assist others in more perilous conditions, such as those on the lifeboats retaining water. These individuals were welcomed onto safer boats as rescue approached.

As the sun rose, it became evident that ice surrounded the survivors, with over twenty icebergs seen in the area. Passengers from the lifeboats were welcomed aboard as those on the *Carpathia* watched in awe. Some of the stronger survivors climbed up on their own, while others had to be carried via slings. It took five hours for all survivors to make it onto the ship. *Mount Temple* and the *Californian* arrived shortly after to search for more survivors, but none were found. Meanwhile, the *Carpathia* changed its route, heading towards nearby New York to ensure the survivors could receive proper care.

Upon arriving in New York, survivors were greeted by thousands of onlookers. Memorials were already being planned in various cities, including Southampton, Belfast, and New York. Ceremonies to honor the survivors were also in the works for the next day or so. Efforts were underway to raise money to support survivors and the families of the deceased. People began questioning the situation, seeking answers about how an unsinkable ship could sink and why there were so few lifeboats. This questioning was led, in part, by the survivors themselves, many of whom felt they had been misled about the safety of the vessel.

As survivors reached dry land, ships began gathering the bodies, discovering over three hundred in total. Some were brought home for funerals, while others were laid to rest at sea. Unfortunately, most of the bodies were lost to the ship and the sea. Southampton experienced an intense period of mourning after the recovery mission, as many late crew and passengers hailed from the city, resulting in a significant loss of citizens. Open weeping was a common sight in the area. Similar conditions prevailed in Belfast, where even the most stoic shipyard workers openly shed tears.

The Aftermath

After the sinking, significant changes were implemented in the sea travel industry. Inquiries into the event were launched by both the United States and Great Britain. The inquiry results attributed some blame to regulations. To prevent similar disasters in the future, several recommendations were made, leading to changes in regulations. These alterations focused on both crash prevention and response.

One huge change was the creation of the International Ice Patrol. This group was a part of the United States Coast Guard tasked with tracking icebergs. They would do this via regular patrols of iceberg-ridden areas and via gaining information from other vessels in these areas.

Lifeboats were a key concern. Part of the tragedy could have been avoided had more lifeboats been readily available. Both authoritative boards in America and Europe declared that future ships should have enough lifeboats aboard to hold all passengers at once. In addition, lifeboat drills would become a required practice and lifeboat inspections would become a part of the pre-voyage process. All of these elements were written into the International Convention for the Safety of Life at Sea, which was a law passed in 1914. This Convention has been changed as needed since then to accommodate changes in travel.

The United States also passed another law in response to the disaster. The Radio Act of 1912 was enacted to prevent communication-related disasters. This law mandated that radio devices on ships must be operational at all times and equipped with backup power supplies to ensure no emergency communications would be missed. Additionally, the act required ships in the same location to maintain contact and made them responsible for communication without relying solely on onshore radio stations. Both acts declared the firing of red flares from a ship as a sign of distress to prevent misinterpretation.

During this time period, the ship *Scotia* was designated as a special weather ship around the Newfoundland area. Its specific task was to  search for icebergs and report their locations via telegraph when found. This information would then be shared with all passing ships to alert them to potential hazards.

However, the inquiries also attributed some blame to the crew of the *Titanic*. Captain Smith failed to take proper precautions after being warned about the icy conditions. The ship's emergency plan had not been fully thought out, prepared, or practiced. Additionally, the crew made a poor decision by proceeding at full speed in conditions with low visibility and weather hazards. However, because such actions were common standards of the time, the companies involved in the voyage were not held responsible. Many ships before had chosen similar actions without facing consequences. Instead, the incident was deemed an unavoidable "Act of God." The only way to prevent a recurrence was by updating the laws appropriately.

The Legacy in Media

The tragedy of the *Titanic* has inspired the media for decades. From non-fiction documentaries about the ship to Hollywood movies fictionalizing the event, the *Titanic* is a common interest to society.

Immediately after the tragedy, poetry about the sinking began to be submitted to newspapers worldwide. Elegies written in verse were published in various papers and some poets released collections dedicated to the events. While some of the poetry was beautiful and heartbreaking, many of the poems sent to newspapers were amateur at best. These poems proved to be an annoyance to publishers of the time. Themes in these poems varied, ranging from the sacrifice of chivalry—citing the men on board who gave up their lives for others—to reflections on the power of nature over man.

Musical pieces about the event followed shortly after the publication of poetry. Over one hundred songs concerning the sinking were created in the year following the event. These were primarily published as sheet music pieces and gramophone records. Notably, the event inspired a significant amount of music from the Southern United States, with several bluegrass and blues songs written about the sinking. The most famous song written about the tragedy, however, was the work of American singer Bob Dylan. The song, titled "Tempest," is the ninth track on his 2012 album of the same name.

The tragedy also permeated African-American culture through music and folklore. Many songs were written, depicting the event as an example of white man's folly. In folklore, it became a legend that a black man had warned the captain of the sinking long before anyone else noticed the damage. Supposedly, this man was ignored due to his skin color and the ship sank due to the crew's ignorance. This character is named "Shine," and much of the story is a play on his name. In the end, he can swim to safety while nobody else can.

Several books have also been written about the event. Among the first to publish written works about the ship were survivors of the disaster. Lawrence Beesley and Archibald Gracie both wrote memoirs concerning the event, containing interviews with other individuals involved, and these works were published rapidly. Books written by various crew members followed soon after. Soon, authors of all varieties began to publish literature on the disaster. However, many of these pieces were inaccurate and heavily exaggerated the events.

Books published long after the sinking of the *Titanic* were found to be more historically accurate. Walter Lord published *A Night to Remember* in the 1950's. This book was significantly more accurate than early books about the ship and quickly became popular. It contained accounts from several survivors and information from historical records. Later, the discovery of the wreckage in the 1980s led to the publication of further books on the topic. Every so often, another event prompts a chain of releases written about the disaster.

Science fiction television has taken a particular interest in the sinking of the *Titanic*. It often appears as a time-travel destination or as part of a larger conspiracy in episodes of appropriately themed shows. In addition, cartoon sitcoms often reference the disaster for comedic effect as a form of black comedy.

The most popular piece of media about the ship is the drama film, *Titanic*, starring Leonardo Dicaprio and Kate Winslet.

The movie follows the exploits of two passengers aboard the ship: Jack Dawson, a third-class passenger who won his ticket via gambling, and Rose Bukater, a rich first-class passenger traveling with her fiancé. The story consists of the two falling in love despite their class differences, only to be torn apart during the tragic sinking of the ship. The film highlights the mingling of classes and the luxury of the ship, as well as the true horror of the sinking.

One interesting medium that has adapted the story is video games. Several video games have been created, either using the disaster as a theme or drawing inspiration from the ship itself. Some games use the sunken ship as a location for a single level, as seen in the video game *Duke Nukem: Zero Hour*. Others, like *Titanic: Adventure Out of Time*, set the entire game alongside the disaster.

The Cultural Impact

The cultural impact of the sinking of the RMS *Titanic* is broad, ranging from the creation of legend to the founding of memorials and museums. The tragedy is both intriguing, frightening, and harrowing to humanity. Even now, over one hundred years later, it continues to impact us.

Several legends surrounding the sinking emerged shortly after the disaster. The most notable example is the notion that the ship was referred to as "unsinkable." In reality, no such explicit claim was made. Instead, Harland & Wolff emphasized safety in their advertising for the ship. Some promotional items stated that the ships were designed to be as unsinkable as technology would allow. Essentially, the claim was that the ships were made to be the best possible, not that they were truly impervious to damage.

The most popular legend focuses on the ship's band. Many survivors stated that the band played until their deaths when the ship began to sink. Some claimed they even moved locations to continue playing as more of the ship went into the water. According to various sources, the last song played before the band perished was the hymn "*Nearer, my God, to Thee.*" However, most of these sources have been debunked as having left the ship long before the band finished playing. It is unknown exactly what the last song played by the band was. However, one man who was rescued at the very last moment stated that all of their music sounded cheerful, even to the bitter end.

Another legend states that the sinking of the *Titanic* marked the first time the "SOS" distress code was used. However, this is untrue. In reality, several vessels had used the code before the *Titanic*. Most simply preferred to use a different code that was common during this era. The *Titanic*, in fact, used a mix of both codes when sending out their distress calls.

One of the most insidious legends to emerge was that of the "*Titanic* curse." Religious figures blamed the White Star Line for the sinking, asserting that it was God's will as the line supposedly did not christen ships. This belief stemmed from a feud between Protestants and Catholics in Belfast, the area where the ship was built. Individuals on both sides accused the White Star Line of favoring one group over the other, resulting in God cursing the ship. However, there is no record of any of these claims being accurate.

On a lighter note, the heroic efforts of a dog on board also became a legend. However, this legend was rooted in fact. A Newfoundland dog named Rigel helped rescue several people during the sinking. Rigel was the dog of William McMaster Murdoch, the ship's First Officer. His barks aided the RMS *Carpathia* in finding the survivors of the sinking. Reportedly, Rigel survived, while his owner did not. He was later adopted by a crew member from the *Carpathia*.

Beyond legends, the public also reacted by creating numerous memorials for the lost victims of the tragedy. These memorials were built in multiple locations and across various nations. Areas with a high number of victims were especially likely to erect monuments or hold memorials for the lost. Two key cities on the ship's route, Southampton and New York, both erected large memorials. Additionally, Belfast erected a memorial due to the city's role in the creation of the ship.

Several other cities also participated in memorial buildings. United Kingdom cities that erected memorials for the victims of the RMS *Titanic* sinking include Colne, Glasgow, Godalming, Lichfield, Liverpool, and London. United States cities that erected memorials include Libertytown, Boston, Washington D.C., and Audubon. In Australia, Broken Hill in New South Wales and Ballarat in Victoria also built memorials.

Museums were also constructed to educate people about the event. In addition, existing museums developed *Titanic*-themed exhibits, with many of them located in the United States. In Branson, Missouri, a large museum is housed in a replica of the *Titanic* (although the replica is only half the size of the original ship) and is simply named "The Titanic Museum." A similar attraction in Pigeon

Forge, Tennessee, was built by the same company. Furthermore, the Titanic Historical Society operates a museum in Indian Orchard, Massachusetts, also named "The Titanic Museum." In Florida, an attraction called "Titanic: The Experience" is located in the city of Orlando, featuring recreations of the maiden voyage with special actors.

Outside of the United States, the SeaCity Museum in Southampton, the Merseyside Maritime Museum in Liverpool, and the Ulster Folk and Transport Museum all have *Titanic*-based artifacts and exhibits. In Belfast, a special attraction was opened specifically to provide information about the ship. The National Maritime Museum has a *Titanic* collection as well. In Nova Scotia, Halifax's Maritime Museum of the Atlantic also features a *Titanic* display, containing actual items from the ship.

The tragedy of the *Titanic* led to an additional incident in June 2023. A crew of five individuals entered into a submersible known as the *Titan* in an attempt to visit the shipwreck of the *Titanic*. The main vessel connected to the submersible lost communication with the vehicle on June 18, 2023. Many feared that the individuals aboard were alive, slowly losing oxygen as time passed. A massive search for the submersible began, lasting days. Finally, wreckage from the submersible was found.

It was determined that the submersible imploded due to the use of carbon fiber, a brittle material used in the construction of the tubular capsule. The crew likely received warnings from the submersible's sensors before hearing creaking noises coming from the hull and losing communication with the main vessel. After failed attempts to surface, the submersible likely entered into a free fall before imploding minutes later. All those aboard died immediately upon implosion. It was later revealed that militaries around the world were aware of the implosion as it happened. This sparked outrage, as a significant amount of time and money had been spent searching for survivors.

This event led to an increase in *Titanic*-based social media posts. Many conspiracy theorists attempted to draw connections between the myths and legends of the *Titanic* and the tragedy of the *Titan*. Others started creating memes and other humorous content centered around the two tragedies. This content revolved around ideas such as ghosts from the *Titanic* meeting new people thanks to the *Titan* imploding, as well as the perceived link between the deaths of those on the luxury ship and the billionaires on the submersible. Many felt these jokes were in poor taste.

Despite the horrors of the sinking, there are rumors that an individual is seeking to build a replica ship that will set sail sometime in the next few decades. This ship will be named *Titanic II*. It is unknown at what point in the process the project is, as it supposedly began in 2012, and no updates have been given.

Conclusion

The sinking of the RMS *Titanic* on April 15, 1912, is one of the most harrowing events in the history of sea travel, resulting in the deaths of over 1,500 people out of approximately 2,224 passengers and crew on board. The disaster could have been entirely avoided and managed properly had the resources been made available.

The ship itself was an impressive vessel of the White Star Line, larger and more luxurious than any ship before it. It could accommodate a multitude of passengers, crew members, workers, and luggage. With ample cargo space and numerous amenities, it provided a comfortable experience for everyone on board. Even third-class passengers were afforded luxuries, including private cabins and social areas.

However, the standards of the time, combined with the hubris of the ship's designers and crew, led to a tragedy that changed history. Adhering to the standards of the era, Captain Smith steered the ship directly into an iceberg at full speed. Failing to prepare for a potential sinking, the crew was left in confusion and chaos while attempting to maintain ship operations and assist passengers in boarding lifeboats. Miscommunications resulted in less than half of the lifeboats' capacities being used, leading to the needless loss of many lives on the ship.

The third class suffered the most casualties because their cabins were located in the most risky area of the ship. In addition, the segregation methods used to keep the classes separate made it harder for them to escape. Yet, the men of the other two classes fared just as poorly, as unclear communication led to them being denied seats on lifeboats.

Those who ended up in the water died quickly as those in lifeboats watched. Despite being rescued by the *Carpathia*, the survivors were forever changed by the event. Many were greatly upset and felt betrayed.

The world reacted with sorrow. Memorials and museums appeared overnight to showcase remembrance of victims and support for survivors. Maritime laws underwent immediate investigations and were changed to reflect the events of the sinking. The media ran with the story, publishing both fiction and non-fiction works immediately after the event.

The world has not yet forgotten the *Titanic*. From music to movies, the story is retold regularly with an intrigue and enthusiasm that is hard to match. The themes of luxury, inter-class mingling, and avoidable tragedy still captivate humanity. Modern attempts to visit the wreckage site have proved to be equally as dangerous, yet humanity cannot seem to resist the allure of the sunken ship.

References

Beesley, Lawrence. *The Loss of the S.S. Titanic: Its Story and Its Lessons.* Europäischer Hochschulverlag (2015)

Dodd, Sophie. *The Titanic: Looking Back at the Ship's Tragic History.* People (2023). https://people.com/human-interest/the-titanic-a-history-of-its-sinking/. Accessed December 01, 2023.

Main, Douglas. *The Titanic: The true story behind the 'unsinkable' ship.* Live Science (2023). https://www.livescience.com/38102-titanic-facts.html. Accessed December 05, 2023.

Maltin, Tim and Aston, Eloise. *101 Things You Thought You Knew About the Titanic ... But Didn't!* Penguin Publishing Group (2011).

River, Charles. *The Titanic: The History and Legacy of the World's Most Famous Ship from 1907 to Today.* CreateSpace Independent Publishing Platform (2017).

Stone, Daniel. *The Unique Combination of Factors That Made the Titanic Become So Famous.* Slate (2023). https://slate.com/news-and-politics/2023/06/titanic-history-how-the-ship-became-so-famous.html. Accessed November 29, 2023.

Sweeney, Michael S. and National Geographic. *Titanic: Uncovering the Secrets of the World's Greatest Shipwreck.* National Geographic Society (2012).

Tikkanen, Amy. *Titanic.* Britannica (2023). https://www.britannica.com/topic/Titanic. Accessed December 03, 2023.

Bonus!

Thanks for supporting me and purchasing this book! I'd like to send you some freebies. They include:

- The digital version of *500 World War I & II Facts*

- The digital version of *101 Idioms and Phrases*

- The audiobook for my best seller *1144 Random Facts*

Scan the QR code below, enter your email and I'll send you all the files. Happy reading!

Find more of me on Amazon!

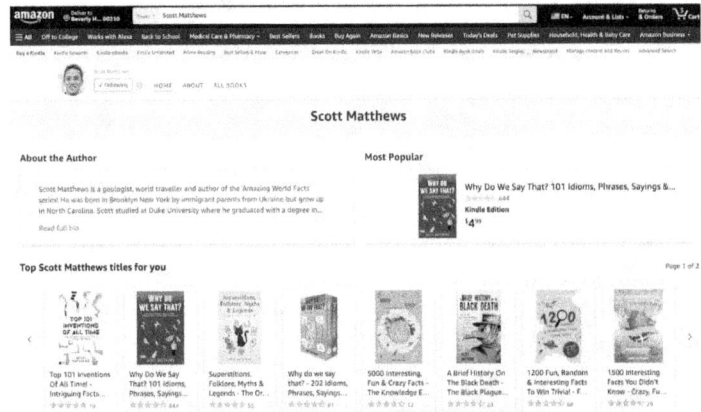

Check out the "Amazing Facts" series and learn more about the world around us!

Check out the "Why Do We Say That" series and learn where everyday idioms and phrases come from!

www.ingramcontent.com/pod-product-compliance
Lightning Source LLC
Chambersburg PA
CBHW052103110526
44591CB00013B/2334